Ghost Hometowns

ALSO BY GIADA NIZZOLI

Will-o'-the-Wisps

Set in Marble

ghost hometowns
Giada Nizzoli

QUERENCIA

Querencia Press, LLC
Chicago, Illinois

ISBN 978 1 959118 13 8

www.querenciapress.com

First Published in 2023

Querencia Press, LLC
Chicago IL

Printed & Bound in the United States of America

CONTENTS

Introduction

There was a small village that was part of the province of Verona, in Northern Italy. However—just between the two of us—it was too far from the city center for me to say that I lived in Verona without feeling guilty of cheating. My parents had moved there from Tuscany around twenty-two years before their marriage dissipated like that area's notorious fog.

There was also Carrara, a town right between the Mediterranean Sea and some marble mountains. A place that most definitely didn't look like your typical, hilly Tuscan landscapes. We'd spend our summer holidays there every year, and my mother gave me a chance to visit Carrara even more often by moving back eventually.

My two hometowns.

And, after moving abroad and starting to visit them through the eyes of someone who no longer lived there, my *ghost* hometowns.

This book is for anyone who has ever experienced the disorienting feeling of not knowing where they belong; of getting tricked by nostalgia while living abroad or far from where they grew up; of not feeling at home in their town, country, or even with their own family due to their racist, homophobic, or misogynistic views.

For you, too.

Unexpected pregnancy

Italy is my mother,
but she had me by mistake.

A stunning single parent
who got pregnant at sixteen
and decided to keep me,
even though deep down she knew
she could not give me the world.

She rocked me in crystal waves
and brought me up amidst the scent
of ripe, yellow citrus fruits
to distract me from the reek
of hazy unemployment
and the gas of corruption.

As I grew, she realized
that I was far too much work.
'Maybe I was wrong,' she thought.
'Maybe I just wasn't ready.'

So, when she gave me ripe lemons,
I made my own lemonade
with the juice of the sour tears
that I cried when I left her.

Italy is my mother,
but she had me by mistake,

and we love each other,
sì, but only from   afar.

A nineteen-year-long one-night stand

Faint frescoes, red marble, and rumbling water,
missed buses and morning coffee aroma:

you were charming, Verona,
in the humid summer air,
as still as my heart
that no longer dwelt in your alleys.

Believe me! You *were* fascinating,
with your Roman columns
whispers of Medieval secrets,
and the modern breeze that made my dress twirl.

It just happened too quickly:
I was born,
I blacked out,
I opened my eyes,
and I was at your place, somehow.

I *tried* to make it work, reaching for the sun
as I ran on the bridge by the old castle
or standing where Romeo and Juliet met...
but it felt forced,
as fake as her balcony.

It's not you, Verona:
it's me.
My heart was just somewhere else.

Ours was a sober one-night stand
that lasted nineteen years,

and now that we're apart,
I still think of you
with the same smile I reserve
for my teenage crushes
and stolen kisses,

and with the same painful wisdom,
I remind myself that not even
the brightest shades of nostalgia
could have painted over a future
that I knew wasn't mine.

And you, Verona,
you deserve someone
who loves you for what you are:
someone who hasn't been cheating on you
with a bunch of foreign towns
ever since she realized
that the future was in her hands.

The American diner in Tuscany

There was an American diner
in the grim industrial area, crammed
between the town and the harbor.

I went there wearing a carousel
of polka dots, backcombed hair,
and my thirst for the foreign.

The waiter greeted us
in a thick Carrara accent,
rolled every R, and found a 'ooh'
in 'ham-b*ooh*rger'.

The diner had bright, verging-on-tacky interiors,
nostalgic pop culture props,
and the most unapologetic clichés
of the American dream.

They served 'becon' and 'chiken',
and milk-*shakes* that were mispronounced
stressing 'shake' instead of 'milk'.

After a cheese-*cake* that was announced
stressing 'cake' instead of 'cheese',
I left with an understanding smile:

oh, how I recognized the struggle
of forcefully squeezing an intangible dream
into a reality we don't belong to.

Cigarettes & bubble-gum

In the merry-go-round of afternoons
taking the same bunch to the usual bench,
cigarettes replaced bubble-gum
to keep their mouths occupied
when they had nothing to say.

And the vivid dreams and hopes
that they had shared as children
and all those exciting plans
for new beginnings away
dissipated like dull,
  t
h
i
n

  s
m
 o
k
  e
in their gray routine,

or were POPPED by their parents
who had forgotten their own
once they had started replacing
gum with tar.

Po Valley

I wish I could have shared the compliant joy of my peers,
thinking that an artificially lit Sunday at the new shopping center
was worth five or six underpaid days
at a fixed-contract customer service job,
spending eight years learning three languages,
only to read foreign brands on boxes.

Of meeting friends for an al fresco aperitivo
at a ground-floor bar next to a main road
with air-conditioner outdoor units
and gray flats towering above the tables.

Of planning a yearly trip to the usual stale slice
of sea, overcrowded beach, and #TakeMeBack selfies.

Of visiting relatives whose words perpetuate
anachronistic ideas and hurtful stereotypes.

Of being fine with the fact that all villagers,
and even the priest, always know my every move.

But I couldn't.

Whenever I tell people I'm from Northern Italy,
I can almost see the aesthetically pleasing yellow hue
of *Call Me by Your Name* or deceitful Instagram filters
fall into their eyes, as they picture
brochure-worthy pastel houses and green landscapes.

They don't know the in-between, gray reality
of pylons, never-ending guardrails, lingering
unemployment, cheap-looking
outlet stores, and crumbling pavements.

And, because those Po Valley villages are far
from famous tourist destinations,
I guess their fancy travel guidebooks won't give them
the answer to why I left them.

Ironic

Years ago, the council commissioned
a postcard-style painting of Venice
on the new building right opposite my childhood house.

Ironic,
if you consider that my mother
had always wanted to visit that place
and that, as a family, we never did.

Ironic,
if you consider that we lived
less than an hour and a half away
from the iconic floating city.

My father knew she was dying to go
but never took her in his car.
My mother obviously knew she was dying to go
but never took a train there.

When we were still a family,
we weren't known for being
the most spontaneous or adventurous
in the village, I guess.

Our weeks blending
into the same year, years feeling
like a mere repetition, and everything
having to be meticulously planned
in advance, of course.

So, can you imagine when their only child
—whose bedroom actually happened to be
right opposite that painting of Venice—

decided she was tired of deceptions
and would have only ever settled
for the real thing, moving abroad
without even planning it in advance?

Ironic,
they thought dreams belonged
in drawers and backs of wardrobes,
but I got tired of them smelling
like mildew and naphthalene.

That itch in the brain

It's the wet gum on the last train seat,
pylons slicing the sunset ahead,
the rubbish by the side of the street,
cold feet sticking out of a warm bed,
racist jokes with a family meal,
the weeds in a tidy flower bed:

when I'm in my home country but feel
like I'm meant to be elsewhere instead.

Swallows & house sparrows

Sometimes I find myself wishing—*no*,
not that I had decided to stay,
as that would have been less realistic
than expecting our local swallows to ignore
that tingling sensation in their quivering feathers
after the last August sunset—

I just find myself wishing
that my old village could have been enough,
for me back then,
like the cozy cracks in buildings
for sedentary house sparrows.

The local bar, the Sunday mass where most
of my friends would meet, helping
organize the September funfair, and only
ever hearing the same dialect,
over and over again.

Because, if it had been enough, then staying
wouldn't have even been a question,
and most definitely not
such a soul-crushing thought.

Do swallows secretly envy house sparrows
when they ready themselves to leave everything
behind?

The girl who used to gaze at Battersea Power Station

I miss the girl who used to gaze
at Battersea Power Station
every time she'd take the train
from the London suburbs to Waterloo and back,
while listening to Pink Floyd on her own
without feeling lonely.

We look a lot alike, and I still wear
her *The Dark Side of the Moon* t-shirt
from time to time,
but we're no longer the same person.

Her love for the birth country of Pink Floyd
still felt reciprocated,
because it hadn't been compromised
by a political change built
against foreign souls like hers,
not just yet.

She hadn't learned to put herself first
to survive in the modern jungle,
not just yet.

So, she was caring
—clueless,
but caring.

And now Battersea Power Station has lost
the charming, abandoned feel
that characterized the brick walls
immortalized on the *Animals* cover.

But, maybe, there's a universe
where it still looks the same,
and that political change never happened,
and the girl who used to gaze
at Battersea Power Station
still exists, is still caring,
and still feels welcome
in the birth country of Pink Floyd.

And, maybe, their music plays in the background
whenever she boards that same train.

Having a coffee with an acquaintance abroad

You both smile and call each other friends
even though this is only the third
time you've met up. You pick a cute café
and sit outside, even though it's surrounded
by traffic and noise and gray
buildings and skies. You start talking.

And everything is fine. You smile.
No: you *laugh.* And you can relate to that random
story they shared. Man, it's like
you've known each other since forever!
Oh, they take two sugars? So do you,
of course. 'But you're already
sweet enough,' they say. And when
is your next day off? You should totally
plan something together.

But then you lift your eyes from the coffee
—the impeccable latte art on its surface
already destroyed—
and it all hits you at once:

the smog that's so different
from the sun-kissed cobblestones
of your old home; the huge, concrete
and glass buildings; the fact that this acquaintance
has been mispronouncing your name but now
it's too late to say anything. And they don't know
your favorite film, and your usual friends
are thousands of miles away, and so is everyone
but you, and you don't really know
what the fuck you're doing here.

So, you breathe. No: get some
          a i r
before diving back.

And you answer your new friend's question
as if nothing had happened.
Shall the two of you take a picture together?
You know, once you crop the cars and add a filter
that replaces all that gray with aesthetically pleasing hues
it'll look like you're having the time of your life,
on Instagram at least.

Wrong choices in London

When the streets and buildings and accents and even dreams are foreign,
your survival instinct might push you to grab onto the wrong person
just because they're as lost as you feel, turning coincidences into
faith, politeness into some admirable gestures, basic decency
into signs of care, and that sticky sensation of dirt into
something you probably shouldn't worry about.

Courage is letting go of their cold hugs
even when you know it'll mean
waking up in such a big,
foreign, alien city
alone.

Only English at work

This British chef at work was raising
his little daughter to be bilingual.
French. Just keep that in mind for later, *oui?*

This other colleague from Algeria—who happened
to speak French more fluently—asked me
what was wrong with me since I
had been off from work for so long,
but he furrowed his brows at all those alien
medical terms in English.

So, since it was just the three of us in the kitchen
and I remembered about this other colleague's daughter,
I assumed it'd be acceptable to explain
my illness in a different language despite
the clause in our contracts, *n'est-ce pas?*

'Oh!' this other guy began, an overly
distressed look on his crossed red and white face.
'Are you two saying bad things about me?'

And I remember my genuine, naïve surprise
and thinking it had to be a joke. After all,
this was before the Brexit referendum
—although I'll let you guess what this chef voted—
so I wasn't that used to not feeling
welcome in this country, not just yet.

'Of course not. You know what we said,'
I laughed. 'You speak French.'
'Not at work,' he specified. 'Only English at work.'

And, as he left, I wondered
how long it would have taken his daughter
to figure out that her father was a *connard*
in both English and French alike.

The Big Ben and I

The Big Ben shone bright through the darkest London night,
a reassuring lighthouse in an impenetrable ocean of strangers,
a beacon of familiarity from all the books and films
that introduced us before I even stood below
its ageless, yellow glow for the first time.

The Big Ben shone bright through the darkest London night,
and I could almost see Peter Pan flying above
all those sleeping roofs and those—wide awake—
of high-street chains and shops with tacky signs, which didn't exist
for as long as I locked eyes with the clock's face.

The Big Ben shone bright through the darkest London night,
and, surely, if I could see it, it meant that I really was the protagonist
of this story. The main character! The one for whom it would've all
worked out in the end somehow. Not many certainties, but at least
I was standing where I was always meant to be.

The Big Ben shone bright through the darkest London night,
but I had to allow the rest of this present-day city to reappear,
as I let a swarm of tourists swallow me
down the closest tube station—second exit to the right—
so that I could then make the last train at Waterloo.

And I reached my overcrowded flat in a far suburb, away
from tourist guides, getting ready for a morning shift
at an hourly rate lower than the price of a coffee and cake.
And *I guess* the Big Ben was still shining bright through that London night,
but I could no longer see it from my bedroom window.

A rented life

Living abroad is a stretched prolongation
of the awkward days or weeks
in between two rented houses,

when the leases overlap
because you needed enough time
to move all of your belongings
and clean up after yourself.

So, you head to the new house
to scrub the floors, and bring
some furniture, and make it
cozy, but no: it still
feels cold and bare.

Then you go back to sleep in the old place,
where your usual bed still is, but
since almost nothing else surrounds it,
all the walls and doors
somehow look different,
even though they haven't really changed,
and it no longer feels like home.

Neither does.

And, because they're both rented,
none of the two actually belongs
to you, anyway.

From afar

Meowing cats staring at the   moon,
birds waving at planes in the   sky,
lighthouses stretching beams at   ships,
hopeless dreamers like you and I:

all cursed to love things   from afar,
pining after them, unaware
about what to do with them if
we eventually get   there.

Nostalgia's dress

As if Nostalgia's signature outfit
weren't distracting enough to interrupt my days,
sometimes she picks that billowy dress
that turns her into an asphyxiating longing
for all the lives I haven't pursued
in my hometown.

Spinning and twirling, she shows them to me
through a kaleidoscope of landscapes,
sea breeze, laughter in the main square,
late-night dinners with friends,
sunsets, dawns, the baker waving at me,
that usual restaurant remembering my table,
and me being happy, despite
not having followed my dreams.

When she walks up and down my street
wearing that billowy dress and puckering her lips,
Nostalgia's charm grows even more irresistible,
and I try reminding myself that—*no*,
that's just her trickery! A hypnotizing illusion.

But she's so breath-taking that I always
end up slipping her some money,
taking her hand, and following her
anyway.

Maps & red flags

One of my home country's maps, that I stow
in that practical but painful space
between my lungs and front ribs,
is that of all my hopeless
what-could-have-beens.

Each city or location has a red flag
—just like the ones I had failed to see
in the people or situations that took me there—
with a different name or idea
written on its floating fabric.

And, although deep down I know
that none of those *what-could-have-beens*
actually stood a chance,
sometimes it still hurts when those flags
brush against my sore lungs.

High-res towns

My brain must be wired to forget
that certain places still exist
even when I'm not there,
unlike in a videogame scenario
where people appear and landscapes
start building themselves only
as the main character gets closer to them:

the waves crashing against the promenade
at dawn, in daylight, when life
feels gloomy in the fog, at sunset,
or under the stars;

my old friend's bedroom with a small shelf
that had basically become mine,
the marble statues overlooking the square,
the bus stop from which new days out would sprout
like ever-changing shoots from the same bud,
or my family's dinner table without my plate.

So, when this system occasionally fails,
I try to tell myself that *yes, sure, of course*
they're already there, but that's simply because
they're constantly waiting for me.

In reality, this unfortunate glitch is another
blatant reminder that life in my hometown
goes on just as smoothly without
my personal aims and side quests.

I'm starting to suspect I was never
player 1 in the first place.

Masochistic nostalgia

Is anyone else addicted
to the nostalgic tightening of the chest
that you only feel whenever
you gaze at or walk past a place
where you've once been unapologetically happy
or, perhaps, even sad
but in a romanticized way?

Streams
of
withered
r
  o
s
  e

w
  a
t
  e
r
falling through my ribs.

Ghost hometowns

Can passersby not see the creeping, colossal cobweb
dangling from the clock tower?
Doesn't the cold air make them shiver
underneath this eerily dark, afternoon sky?
And aren't other villagers' words muffled
when they reach their ears?

As I walk through my ghost hometown,
my fingers feel itchy after running them along
dusty walls and unfamiliar shop signs,
while their owners gaze at me with furrowed brows,
wondering why they've never seen me before.

It's almost as if the others can still perceive
the beauty behind the flaky plaster walls,
attract the warmth of the sun,
immediately recognize everyone's voice,
and, above all, feel themselves being
a part of it all.

Me? No. When I boarded that plane,
I must have been transported
to an unsettling different dimension,
and I'll never see this ghost hometown
in the same way they do,
except when—rarely—I happen to bump
into an exiled villager like me.

Then I can still gaze at my old hometown
—no cobwebs, dust, nor ghosts—
in their eyes.

And they, in mine.

Divorce on a loop

Flying home to see family who now live
in two different towns hundreds of kilometers apart
is just a more marketable way of saying
RELIVING YOUR PARENTS' DIVORCE
ALL OVER AGAIN
FOR TWO WHOLE WEEKS.

I guess the latter wouldn't have looked as appealing
on the brochure that life's tourist office
had handed to me when I first moved abroad.

And that's under-selling it: it's longer than two
if you count the additional weeks
of planning, and all the texts and calls
leading up to what should be a holiday,
as well as scouting for flights to and from
two different airports but returning
to the same one.

'Why are you spending an extra day
with your mother? That's unfair.'

'You must come and say hi
to your great-aunt, then have lunch with uncle:
you don't want to offend them, do you?'

'I can't believe you're seeing your friend
on Wednesday afternoon, too!'

'Well, I've already booked dinner on Thursday,
so you might have to cancel on them.'

And my diary fills up as quickly
as the drumming anxiety and black bile
in my stomach.

Flying home to see family who now live
in two different towns hundreds of kilometers apart
should feel like a double vacation,
but, instead, it's just another (guilt) trip.

Autumn leaf

Just like a stubborn, withered leaf
holding fast to its branch
to defy the cold November breeze,
I still expect my village
to freeze in time while I'm away
and bloom back to life one week a year
every time I manage to visit.

I try and squeeze years of friendships
into short time slots, as if
our old selves could feel the same
in front of a quick coffee
before my next train or bus,

but nothing waits for me, not even
the climbing weeds on the cracked walls
of the abandoned house in the parking lot,
certainly not the Monday market,
nor, of course, my friends.

We've just become so good at pretending
that, sometimes, I might even believe it,
like that leaf wishing the pale November sun
into a summer afternoon.

Family Q&A
[tw: racism]

'Where's the boyfriend?'   when I'm single,
'When's the wedding?'   when I'm not.
'When we were your age,
we already had kids.'
'A steady job.'
'A mortgage.'

'What is it that you do, again?'
'Copywriter? That tiny thing behind
the first pages of a book?'
'Oh, a freelancer. Well, that's not
a real job, now, is it?'
'Your own business, you say?'
'Well, more like a website, though.'

'So, when are you having kids?'
'Hopefully you'll baptize them.
That's important,' they stress.
'It's so sad how your generation
is losing our religious values.'

                                  Then the TV announces
                                  that a refugee has perished
                                  crossing the sea with her baby.

'Good,' they say.
'We haven't got enough room
for them in our country.
They should all drown.'

On leaving

The usual question: 'Why did you leave?'

> Because I already had a long-distance affair
> with a papier-mâché version of England created
> with the backgrounds of Beatles interviews and
> nineteenth-century literature and Quadrophenia scenes.

> I left because anything—whether wiping tables
> or toilets—would have been worth it
> if I could walk down those streets.

> Because the gray reality of my Northern
> Italy village couldn't compete against London's
> kaleidoscope of shops and architecture.

> I left because the possibility to be or reinvent myself
> from scratch sounded more appealing than resurfacing
> from years as an OCD-plagued outsider
> in a bigoted village that was religious
> with judging others.

> I left because I suppose I fancied Italy
> but didn't want us to get too serious:
> after all, I was too young
> to be tied down.

> Because I wanted to miss my home,
> because I wanted to find a new one.

> I left because, if I could just focus
> on 'where', then I wouldn't have needed to worry
> about 'when' or 'what' to do.

Because some relatives said that I couldn't,
because some others said that I wouldn't
have managed.

The usual answer, raising my shoulders: 'More opportunities,
I guess.'

A holiday, but
[tw: racism, homophobia]

N-bombs, F-words—and not
the spontaneous one used
for regular swearing.
'Bloody Romanians, bringing crime
to our beautiful country.'
'Back in my days.'
'When Mussolini was in power.'

'That Greta girl,' they say,
as they put down another load
of single-use plastic bottles,
'why is she so angry, anyway?'

'Therapy is stupid. Have you tried
chamomile for your so-called,'
—inverted commas hanging in the air—
'depression?'

'I'm not a homophobe,'
they say, after I ask them to drop
dropping that F-word. Again.
After all, they have a gay friend,
they'll have me know.

'I'm not racist,'
they insist, and I can already feel
my stomach muscles clench
to deal with the blow of the usual
conjunction... *'but!'*

Going home to see my family
should feel like a holiday   ... but.

Ragdoll

I'm an uncomfortable daughter and relative
to have at a big family dinner:
I no longer keep quiet when they spoon-feed me
N-bombs, patriarchy anthems, and homophobic comments.

Don't get me wrong: I won't argue
against improbable pizza toppings,
films, songs, and the best dog breed
of all time, even though I might
have a different opinion from theirs.

But I won't smile and nod
if everyone believes that 'hate' and 'free'
are the same types of speech, that climate change
is a hoax, and refugees shouldn't
be helped as they die at sea.

Smiling and nodding is enabling,
and keeping quiet is agreeing.

Perhaps I won't change anyone's mind
with my numbers, facts, and empathy,
but they'll know there are consequences
when such things are said out loud.

So, I guess that makes me
an uncomfortable daughter and relative
to have at a big family dinner.

Or, *maybe*, they're disappointed because
they expected a ragdoll in my place.
A quiet one.
Not even a puppet with pre-recorded sounds:
they'd rather not take any risks.

Friendship scrapbook

I created a flesh-and-blood scrapbook
by gluing faded memories together
and filling the gaps with all the information
subconsciously gathered through years
of being silent Facebook friends,

but I can already see the sunlight tearing through
the weakest spots, where the glue hadn't stuck
or the raw material just wasn't enough.

If the way I see them in my head
is not who they have become,
then my old friends can only be ghosts,
but so am I:

the only one who suddenly
disappeared from birthday pictures,
invitations, and one day
—slowly and all at once—
from all their conversations.

We're all ghosts, yet I'm the one
who somehow ended up haunting
a different place, spontaneous meetings
replaced by a yearly séance.

23 kilograms of baggage

Before my international check-in,
I tricked myself into believing
that all my friendships, catchphrases,
and unspoken traditions
were set in stone but light enough
for me to carry them abroad
and then back home again
whenever I visited.

But something felt heavy, and
after a few trips, I realized they went above
the harsh 23 kg limit imposed
by one of the cheapest airlines.

So, just like with that spare dress and straw hat
that I had packed just in case,
I started removing them,
   one
   at
   a
   time,
to obtain a suitcase that wasn't so difficult
to drag behind me.

After a few trips, not much was left
from the baggage I had first packed,

and even though the suitcase is now
undeniably lighter and easier to carry,
it's my chest that feels heavier
whenever I think about it.

Colonnata

When we'd still spend our summers in Carrara as a family,
my father would drive us to Colonnata,
a small 532m-high village surrounded
by marble mountains and marble
quarries and marble benches and marble
artisans and marble souvenir shops with marble
floors and marble columns and marble, marble, marble,
more white than I had ever seen
in one place. It didn't even look real
as I squinted in the sunlight reflected
by the quarries!

We'd go to those marble shops in Colonnata
every single time, since everything we did
as a family was a repetition,
a ritual, a reassuring—back then—
or asphyxiating—when I think about it now—routine,
even on holiday.

So, when years later my mother mentioned
that I had never actually been to Colonnata,
it felt like being told that Santa
wasn't real—spoiler alert.
Apparently, those touristy shops by the quarries
weren't technically Colonnata, she explained.

So, we took the bus there when my boyfriend and I
visited her from the UK, the kind of steep ride
where the driver had to beep the horn
at every impenetrable corner.
And I saw Colonnata for the first time:
it was still full of marble, but less white.

There was draping laundry and purple or yellow flowers
on balconies and inns and bars
and locals chatting in a different dialect.
We sat al fresco at a wobbly table in the shade
and ordered four *focacce* stuffed with Colonnata's
world-famous *lardo*, white like its marble
but much softer and more flavorful to savor.
The down-to-earth owner of that *larderia* admitted
to not having enough lard to stuff four,
so he offered to make us a special
sharing platter instead.

That was Colonnata.

And, as the owner brought out some bread baskets
and a wooden board covered with local produce,
I wondered just how many things and places
I had been missing out on
by sticking to the same routine.

A doomed quest

Where's home? The rented flat with my name
next to the cobweb-covered bell,
to which I sometimes get takeaways delivered
and still don't know my neighbor's name?

No, every motivational quote online will tell you
—a clashing of fonts against an overused stock image—
that home isn't a place, silly:
it's *people*.

But who?

Now that the anachronistic myth
of the happy community in its own bubble
has been burst, I no longer have the luxury
of finding all my loved ones
where they were when I was a child.

Different villages, towns, countries,
and even ways of looking at life,
and whenever I visit them
—separately, one or two at a time—
I feel like a slightly different version
of myself, twisting my movements,
voice, and personality into what *they*
were used to, so as not to scare them.

But then, if they're scattered all over the place
and I have to refrain from being myself,
surely home can't be people either.

So, how exactly can I find it
if I don't actually know
what on earth to look for?

Fuck-towns

To spare myself from heartache,
I had learned to love places
in the same way I loved fuckboys:
        unconditionally,
        and not at all,
making the most of those strong
but ephemeral sensations
yet accepting that they could have never
given me what I needed
nor made me feel complete.

Echoes of cicadas

Perhaps the cicadas do sing more harmoniously
when I remember those summer seasons
through nostalgia's distorted lenses.
The sticky nudge of the hair against my neck
during those scorching hot afternoons
is replaced by a pleasant, warm breeze.
The buses skipping a ride every other day
become impeccable, and their windows
filled with wonders, even though I'd listen to music
or check my phone most of the time.

And yes, I suppose I forget about waiting hours
after a meal and needing time to face the cold shore,
convincing myself that I used to be one with the sea.
All the arguments and misunderstandings
with friends, and that time I mistook curiosity
for falling in love, they're all blurred:
after all, the pictures on my phone only show me
staged smiles and laughter.

But the tingling flavor of freedom after years
in a home where even a food shopping
had to be planned and routines were carved
too deep in stone to make room
for unpredictable and spontaneous whims,
that wasn't amplified by nostalgia:

will I ever experience it again,
or has my parents' stone-carving gene
already been activated
underneath my skin?

A cozy déjà vu

Perhaps home is no longer a place
nor a person in themself:

it's a rare moment of coziness,
a déjà vu of the senses
that you can occasionally experience
when you spend time with someone
with whom walls aren't needed,
usually—but not always—
in a familiar place,

and for the seconds or hours it lasts,
you don't find yourself wishing
that you were somewhere else instead.

Notes on Previous Publications

Unexpected pregnancy – October Hill Magazine

Earlier versions of *Swallows & house sparrows* and *Nostalgia's dress* –
Depression is what really killed the dinosaurs, an anthology by Sunday
Mornings at the River

The girl who used to gaze at Battersea Power Station and an earlier version
of *Ragdoll* – Ink Sac by Cephalopress

CPSIA information can be obtained
at www.ICGtesting.com
Printed in the USA
BVHW031829240223
659186BV00002B/127